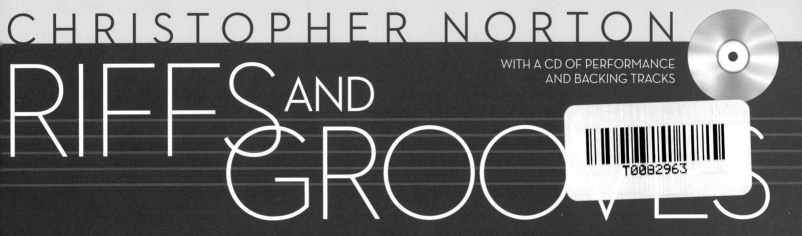

CHRISTOPHER NORTON

RIFFS AND GROOVES

WITH A CD OF PERFORMANCE
AND BACKING TRACKS

T0082963

28 LOWER INTERMEDIATE PIANO PIECES

Producer and performer on the companion CD:
Christopher Norton

Includes selections from these Christopher Norton collections
published by Boosey & Hawkes:

Celtic Melt
Chunky Phunky
Country Comfort
Microjazz Collection 1
Microjazz Collection 2
Microjazz Collection 3
Microstyles Collection
Smooth Groove

BOOSEY & HAWKES

DISTRIBUTED BY

HAL•LEONARD®
CORPORATION
7777 W. BLUEMOUND RD. P.O. BOX 13819 MILWAUKEE, WI 53213

www.boosey.com
www.halleonard.com

CONTENTS

After the Battle

CHRISTOPHER NORTON

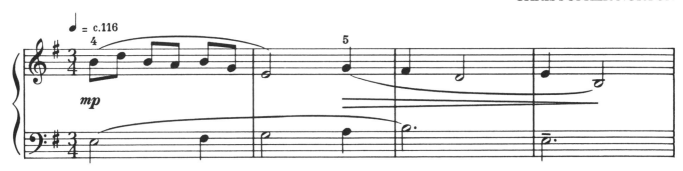

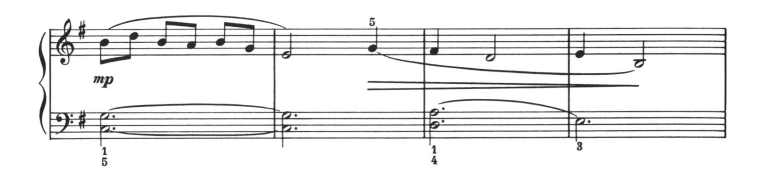

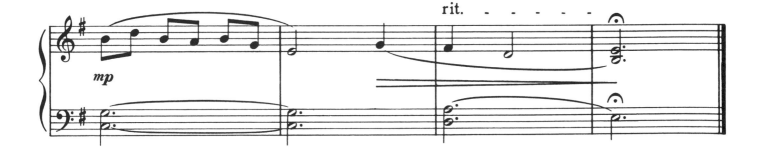

Becalmed

CHRISTOPHER NORTON

Big Jim

CHRISTOPHER NORTON

Blues No. 1

CHRISTOPHER NORTON

A Chromatic Outing
(*Chromatics*)*

CHRISTOPHER NORTON

* Don't hang about! Aim to play the chromatic runs smoothly.

Coconut Rag

CHRISTOPHER NORTON

Down South

(*Rock Ballad*)*

CHRISTOPHER NORTON

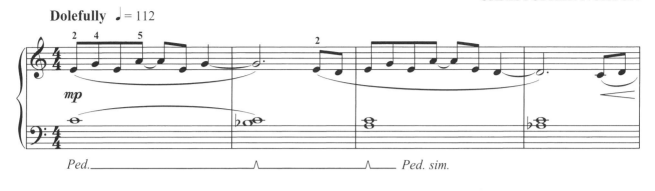

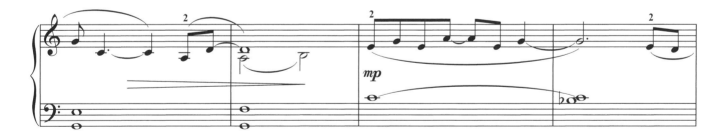

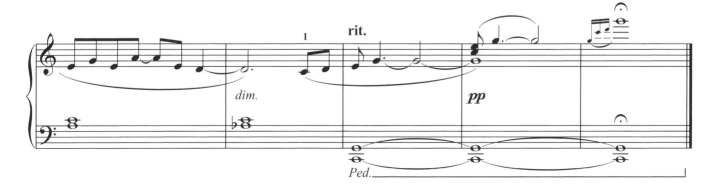

* This style usually takes the form of a lyrical melody line above slow-moving harmonies.

From Far Away

CHRISTOPHER NORTON

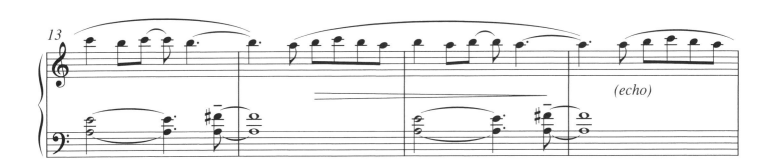

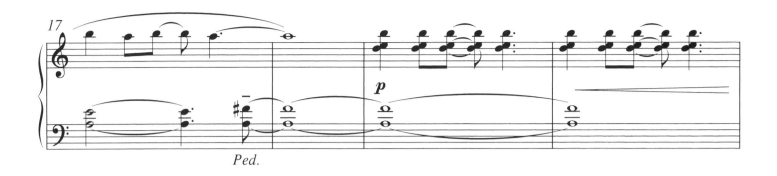

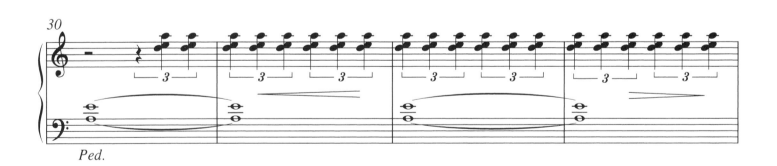

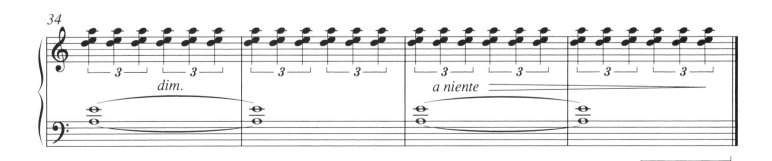

Fax Blues
(*Ostinato*)*

CHRISTOPHER NORTON

* An ostinato is a phrase repeated over and over again. Here it is in the left hand, while the right hand moves freely with an air of improvisation.

Get in Step

CHRISTOPHER NORTON

Hideaway
(*Rumba*)*

CHRISTOPHER NORTON

Simply ♩ = 126

* The rumba is of Cuban origin but became a popular dance in the USA and Europe in the 1930s, where it absorbed elements of jazz.

Inter-city Stomp

CHRISTOPHER NORTON

Metal Merchant
(*Heavy Metal*)*

CHRISTOPHER NORTON

* This is an aggressive style of rock music based around electric guitars and drums.

Mists among the Stones

CHRISTOPHER NORTON

Misty Day
(*Waltz*)*

CHRISTOPHER NORTON

* A gentle dance: think of one beat per bar to keep it moving.

Not Sorry Enough

CHRISTOPHER NORTON

Open Space

CHRISTOPHER NORTON

Reflections

CHRISTOPHER NORTON

for Rex Billingham

Reggae

CHRISTOPHER NORTON

Road Racer

CHRISTOPHER NORTON

for Rex Billingham

A Sad Song

CHRISTOPHER NORTON

Shamrock Flyer

CHRISTOPHER NORTON

Take your Time

CHRISTOPHER NORTON

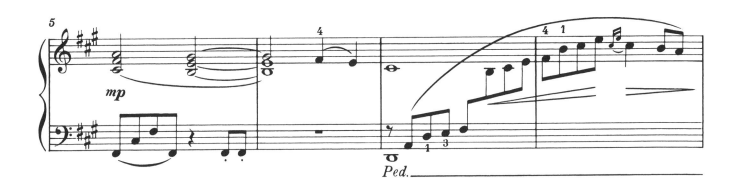

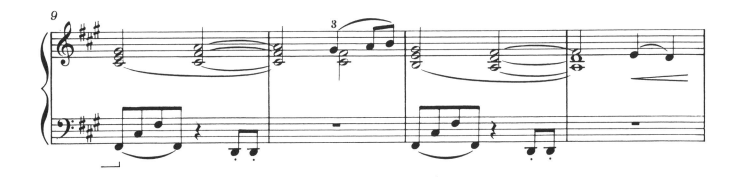

A Short Walk

CHRISTOPHER NORTON

Three plus Two Blues

Lively (♩ = c.160)

CHRISTOPHER NORTON

Two-handed Blues

CHRISTOPHER NORTON

White Rose City

CHRISTOPHER NORTON

A Winter Song

CHRISTOPHER NORTON